Table of Contents

Subject Matter	Pages
Lesson 1: Board Member Duties	2-4
Lesson 2: Becoming a Transparent Board	5-9
Lesson 3: Conflicts of Interest in the HOA	10-11
Lesson 4: Understand the Governing Documents	12-13
Lesson 5: Business 101: Planning The Operation Plan & Project Management	14-21
Lesson 6: The Association's 3P's: Practices	22-24
Lesson 7: The Association's 3P's: Processes	25-30
Lesson 8: The Association's 3P's: Procedures/Policies	31-34
Lesson 9: Selecting the Association Management Company	35-44
Future Topics	45
References	46-47
Author Information	48
Legal Review	49

9 Lessons the Board Member Needs to Know

*Do the **right** things*
*At the **right** time*
*By the **right** people*

Today's buyers are savvy and smart investors. The smart home buyers will avoid buying into Associations where common areas are not presentable and community budgets show cost overruns and special assessments for unplanned repairs. Therefore the Board of Directors (BOD) of the Homeowners Association (HOA) and the Management Company have to be a team; for none can do it alone. It is a three way street! The HOA Board has to understand why things must be done in a certain way. The Board member may have to change his or her paradigm and begin understanding that an HOA is a business. In doing that the Board member has to understand the duties he or she has to the other members on the board, the homeowners and the people who work for the Association.

The Management Company works for the Board of Directors.
The Board of Directors work for the Homeowners.
They all have some level of fiduciary duties.

Lesson 1: Board Member Duties

When a homeowner decides to run for the Board of Directors (BOD) of their Homeowners Association (HOA) they need to understand what is expected of them and the duties that will be required. There are many duties a board member is responsible for, but at the core is a duty of trust; better known as a fiduciary duty. The State of South Carolina has defined a fiduciary relationship as one in which a party "reposes special confidence in another so that the latter, in equity and good conscience, is bound to act in good faith and with due regard to the interests of one reposing the confidence.[1]" Amongst those duties of trust in regards to BOD are a Duty of Care, Duty of Loyalty, Duty to Act with the Scope of Authority, and the Duties as a Board Officer. The duties of a board officer are found under **SC Code § 33-31-842.**

Standards of conduct for officers.

(a) An officer with discretionary authority shall discharge his duties under that authority:

(1) in good faith;

(2) with the care an ordinarily prudent person in a like position would exercise under similar circumstances; and

(3) in a manner the officer reasonably believes to be in the best interests of the corporation, and its members, if any.

While the concept of fiduciary duty is somewhat amorphous, the Court has used its' discretion to help it apply to many situations. It is these duties that are the core of what a BOD is to abide by. If not they are often the ones that result in legal consequences because of a breach of duties. Breach of duties occur when a board member abuses his or her power by repose of trust or confidentiality that results in harm to one or more of his or her constituents. The constituents include fellow board members, homeowners, and staff members of the management company, businesses you do business with or those that provided confidential bids. Let me simplify it further by breaking down the meanings of each word as defined in the Webster Dictionary. This will better assist you in understanding the contexts of the explanation.

---

[1] *Hendricks v. Clemson Univ.,* 339 S.C. 552, 529 S.E.2d 293 (Ct. App. 2000).

Definition of fiduciary
Noun fi·du·cia·ry
: One that holds a fiduciary relation or acts in a fiduciary capacity

Definition of duty
Noun du·ty
: Something that is done as part of a job
: Something that you must do because it is morally right or because the law requires it

Definition of constituent
Noun con·stit·u·ent
: Any one of the people who live and vote in an area: a member of a constituency
: One of the parts that form something
: One who authorizes another to act as an agent

The Board of Directors in an HOA wear many hats!

Primary "Hat" is the one with the fiduciary responsibility to the homeowners–that of Duty of Care, Duty of Loyalty, Duty of Authority, and Duty as an Officer in the HOA.

Secondary "Hat" and ON comes into play because <u>the Board member has a duty to protect the HOA from lawsuits.</u> Therefore, must act within the law when conducting business with third-party constituents (members and agents), and has a <u>level</u> of fiduciary (business capacity) and duty (to conduct business morally and ethically within the law). Third party constituents can include the agents from the Management Company (if one exist) Insurance Brokers, Attorneys, Contractors Bidding within the Community, Contractors working within the Community, and the Homeowners. The homeowner becomes a third-party constituent when HOA business, for example late payment, rule violation, etc., is discussed and that information is private and should not be made privy to the entire HOA only the BOD.

Primary Fiduciary Duty to Homeowners

Duty of Care
Requires you to act in good faith and make informed decisions
Act with moral accountability at all times in an ethical and fair manner. Use sound business judgment to protect the fiscal and structural security of the building(s), the Association and the well-being of visitors and homeowners.

Duty of Loyalty
Requires you to put the interest of the association above your personal interest
To hold confidential from any third party constituent any information and communication between the board and an attorney, companies contractually doing business or providing bids for the Association and business pertaining to other homeowners. To be loyal and respect your fellow board members in and out of the boardroom. To not participate in fostering a culture of secret sounding boards and gossip within the community.

Duty to Act within the Scope of Authority
Requires you to perform only those duties you're obligated to carry out
The authority of an HOA comes from its obligations under state laws, as well as the authority granted to it in the governing documents; therefore, the board can only perform the duties, decisions or actions they have the authority to execute.

Duties on the Board

Position	Duties
President	<ul><li>Determines the overall goals of the association</li><li>Must completely understand the governing documents</li><li>Needs to understand the associations financial position</li><li>Confirms that the association is adequately insured</li><li>Responsible for developing committee volunteers to assist</li><li>Maintains a close work relationship with the property manager</li><li>Operates the meeting and keeps order</li></ul>
Vice President	<ul><li>Operates as the President in the Presidents absence</li><li>If acting President he or she will have all the powers and duties of the association president.</li></ul>
Secretary	<ul><li>Takes minutes at meetings and responsible for recording meetings</li><li>Sends notices and keeps the association members informed</li><li>Responsible for maintaining all records of the association</li><li>Updates and maintains the governing documents, policies and rules and regulations</li><li>Responsible for the storage and/or disposing of old records</li></ul>
Treasurer	<ul><li>Reviews the financial and annual budget</li><li>Signatory on promissory notes</li><li>Signatory on documents that confirm official audits and reviews of the financials by outside accountant</li><li>Gives the financial report at all meetings</li><li>Assures all tax returns are filed on time</li><li>Regularly recommends the reserve study</li></ul>

Lesson 2: Becoming a Transparent Board

When one hears the word *transparent* it means easily detected or seen, readily visible and accessible. In the business world it means much more. Depending on the type of business particular laws and practices dictate just how transparent you can be. In the HOA business environment your bylaws dictate what state laws "act" the community is governed by and the bylaws enacted by the community. The word *transparent* never means to disclose private board business that involves confidential information, trade practices and/or specific business practices privy to the board through a bidding process. That is why the laws have been written to protect confidential information and the protection of free trade practices.

The board should never put the Association in harm of damaging its reputation among the business community. As stated in the fiduciary responsibilities explained above the board has a duty to protect the Association from potential lawsuits and to act in an ethical way that fosters good faith and sound business judgment.

Ways the Board Becomes Transparent

- Express yourself in a clear transparent manner so motives, goals and/or objectives are seen and heard.
- Educate yourself on business practices to understand the concepts of good faith and ethical business practices.
- Conduct business
    - On the table, not under it!
    - In the room and not behind closed doors!
- Lead by example, to provide the future board members sound business practices to follow.
- Be open about your business relationships by revealing Conflicts of Interest.
- Foster "Freedom of Information" by informing the community of what can and cannot be shared, and the instructions on how and when information that can be shared will be available.

Know What Records Can be shared with Homeowners

Notice: Records that are to be shared in South Carolina Code of Laws do NOT include bids and the contents in contracts, for both discuss confidential business practices. Even if a contract does not have a confidentiality clause, which most do, the information should not be subject to examination by homeowners.

Certain records are subject to disclosure in the South Carolina Code of Laws, and below we will discuss accounting records as defined in the Accounting Education Organization.
http://www.accountingedu.org/accounting-records.html

Accounting Records: Records include the accounting system used to record and track financial transactions, prepare financial statements, and the supporting documents, such as checks and invoices.

Basic Record Keeping in Accounting

A basic record keeping system for a business generally consists of:
1. A basic journal for recording transactions, such as revenues and expenses
2. Accounts receivable and accounts payable records
3. Inventory records (In HOA Supplies: Office, Janitorial, Maintenance, etc.)
4. Payroll records
5. Petty cash records (If your HOA uses this system)
6. Records also include tracking of assets and liabilities.

SC Laws in this book were taken from the unannotated South Carolina Code on the General Assembly's website, which is now current through the 2014 session.

Below are some of the Laws your Community may have to follow:

Title 33 - Corporations, Partnerships and Associations
CHAPTER 31.
SOUTH CAROLINA NONPROFIT CORPORATION ACT
ARTICLE 16.
RECORDS AND REPORTS
SUBARTICLE A.
RECORDS

SECTION 33-31-1601. Corporate records.

(a) A corporation shall keep as permanent records minutes of all meetings of its members and board of directors, a record of all actions taken by the members or directors without a meeting and a record of all actions taken by committees of the board of directors as authorized by **Section 33-31-825(d).**

...

(e) A corporation shall keep a copy of the following records at its principal office:
(1) its articles or restated articles of incorporation and all amendments to them currently in effect;
(2) its bylaws or restated bylaws and all amendments to them currently in effect;
(3) resolutions adopted by its board of directors relating to the characteristics, qualifications, rights, limitations, and obligations of members or any class or category of members;
(4) the minutes of all meetings of members and records of all actions approved by the members for the past three years;

(5) all written communications to members generally within the past three years, including the financial statements furnished for the past three years under **Section 33-31-1620;**
(6) a list of the names and business or home addresses of its current directors and officers; and
(7) its most recent report of each type required to be filed by it with the Secretary of State under this chapter.

SECTION 33-31-1602. Inspection of records by members.
(a) Subject to subsection (e) and **Section 33-31-1603(c),** a member is entitled to inspect and copy, at a reasonable time and location specified by the corporation, <u>any of the records of the corporation described in Section 33-31-1601 (e)</u> if the member gives the corporation written notice or a written demand at least five business days before the date on which the member wishes to inspect and copy.
(b) Subject to subsection (e), a member is entitled to inspect and copy, at a reasonable time and reasonable location specified by the corporation, any of the following records of the corporation if the member meets the requirements of subsection (c) and gives the corporation written notice at least five business days before the date on which the member wishes to inspect and copy:
(1) Excerpts from any records required to be maintained under **Section 33-31-1601 (a),** to the extent not subject to inspection under **Section 33-31-1602 (a);**
(2) Accounting records of the corporation; and
(3) subject to **Section 33-31-1605,** the membership list.
(e) The articles or bylaws of a religious corporation may limit or abolish the right of a member under this section to inspect and copy any corporate record.

SECTION 33-31-1603. Scope of inspection rights.
(c) The corporation may impose a reasonable charge, covering the costs of labor and material, for copies of any documents provided to the member. The charge may not exceed the estimated cost of production or reproduction of the records.

SECTION 33-31-1605. Limitations on use of membership list.
Without consent of the board, a membership list or any part of a membership list may not be obtained or used by a person for any purpose unrelated to a member's interest as a member. Without limiting the generality of the foregoing, without the consent of the board a membership list or any part of the list **may not be:**
(1) Used to solicit money or property unless the money or property will be used solely to solicit the votes of the members in an election to be held by the corporation;
(2) Used for any commercial purpose; or
(3) Sold to or purchased by any person.

SECTION 33-31-1620. Financial statements for members.
(a) Except as provided in the articles or bylaws of a religious corporation, a corporation upon written demand from a member or the Attorney General shall furnish the demanding party its latest annual financial statements, which may be consolidated or combined

statements of the corporation and one or more of its subsidiaries or affiliates, as appropriate, that include a balance sheet as of the end of the fiscal year and statement of operations for that year. If financial statements are prepared for the corporation on the basis of generally accepted accounting principles, the annual financial statements also must be prepared on that basis.

(b) If annual financial statements are reported upon by a public accountant, the accountant's report must accompany them. If not, the statements must be accompanied by the statement of the president or the person responsible for the corporation's financial accounting records:

(1) stating the president's or other person's reasonable belief as to whether the statements were prepared on the basis of generally accepted accounting principles and, if not, describing the basis of preparation; and

(2) describing any respects in which the statements were not prepared on a basis of accounting consistent with the statements prepared for the preceding year.

Depending on which state laws your community must abide by, a condominium development follows the Horizontal Property Act.

Title 27 - Property and Conveyances
CHAPTER 31
HORIZONTAL PROPERTY ACT
ARTICLE 1 -GENERAL PROVISIONS

SECTION 27-31-180. Records of receipts and expenditures.
The administrator or the board of administration, or other form of administration specified in the bylaws, shall keep a book with a detailed account, in chronological order, of the receipts and expenditures affecting the property and its administration, and specifying the maintenance and repair expenses of the common elements and any other expenses incurred. Both the book and the vouchers accrediting the entries made thereupon shall be available for examination by all the co-owners at convenient hours on working days that shall be set and announced for general knowledge.

Both acts describe what can be shared and below are the reasons why a board should NOT release bid documents and confidential contents of contracts discussing business practices. Remember, SC Code of Laws do not list these records as those that are subject to examination by homeowners. Therefore, bids or contracts should NOT be posted on the Associations website for viewing by all. See list below.

1. **The HOA records are NOT public records.** The term "public records" pertain to governmental communities, such as municipalities, cities, townships or bureaus, or any entity that receives public government funds.
2. **HOA's are PRIVATE communities.** The copying of records will be explained in the state, county and bylaws the community has adopted.

3. **It is against MANY laws.** State and Federal Laws state that certain records or information may be blocked from view from others because it meets privacy and/or confidentiality exemption. We sometimes hear that the bylaws state we can show records; however, remember that Federal, State and Local laws supersede and the bylaws cannot go against the law.
4. **The Board has a Fiduciary Duty.** The Board has a level of fiduciary duty to the businesses that bid within the community. Laws were written to protect unfair COMPETITION. Information on contracts can involve pricing, material, procedural practices, etc. which would be private and confidential information. Even if the contract does not have a confidentiality clause the board has a fiduciary duty to protect and keep confidential information provided in contracts and/or through bidding processes private. If this information got into the hands of others that it was not intended for, it could result in price fixing, collusion or open competition.
5. **Simply Not ETHICAL BUSINESS PRACTICES:** Contracts and agreements foster mutually beneficial working relationships and ensure an amicable and successful endeavor for both parties.

SC Laws in this book were taken from the unannotated South Carolina Code on the General Assembly's website, which is now current through the 2014 session.

Lesson 3: Conflicts of Interest in the HOA

When dealing with the Board of Directors (BOD) of the Homeowners Association (HOA) the member must first put-aside any prior understanding or experience they had with *Conflicts of Interest* in the corporate world. The rules for *Conflict of Interest* in the HOA dynamics vary and only exist when it pertains to **VOTING.**

Conflicts and Voting

Conflict exists when one is employed by, related to or does business with any business entity with which the business has a contract. Some corporate boards will not even permit a person with a conflict from having a seat on their board. However, a member of an HOA may become a member of the BOD even though he or she has a *Conflict of Interest*.

Although it is good business practice that members of the BOD inform their regime when a *Conflict of Interest* exists, it is the governing documents that will dictate if that is a requirement.

The board member can be involved in all aspects of his or her board position; however, must refrain from **VOTING** when a *Conflict of Interest* exists.

Conflicts and Board Dynamics

HOA's hold elections for seats on the BOD. Some HOA's have multiple regimes and therefore elect a BOD for each regime. The governing documents will explain how board creation is developed within your community. Usually when multiple regimes exist within an HOA a Master Board is composed of appointed "At Large or Delegate" Directors from each regimes BOD.

The Master Board is assigned certain areas to manage to help alleviate the amount of business the regime BOD is dealing with and this is usually the common amenities. The creation of a Master Board is usually operated by the Association. It will have either two monthly assessments, one to your sub (regime) and the other to your Master Board, or one monthly assessment and the sub (regime) will pay a % of the fee to the Master Board. Either way, the Master Board is supported by the Association and operating simply in the capacity of a "Committee"; although they can discuss and solve issues they cannot **VOTE** as individuals. These "At Large/Delegate" Directors present the information back to their regime BOD who will **VOTE** on that issue and the "At Large/Delegate" Director carries that **VOTE** back to the Master Board.

**Therefore, in actuality no Conflict of Interest
Can ever exist on a Master Board because
No VOTING takes place as an Individual!**

If the "At Large/Delegate" Director has a *Conflict of Interest* and he or she abstains from **VOTING** on that issue <u>when it is being voted on within their regimes BOD</u>, the "At Large/Delegate" Director is simply "carrying" his or her regimes BOD **VOTE** back to the Master Board.

Get with the times ---Consider Online Voting!

Lesson 4: Understand the Governing Documents

GAIN KNOWLEDGE: The Board and Homeowner should understand the type of developments in which they live and study the laws that govern them.

Community Association – is a generic term for communities that are created pursuant to recorded covenants or other documents that create an association of the unit or homeowners. They are typically organized as not-for-profit corporations, which is sometimes confused with the non-profit classification. However, if incorporated both classifications follow the SC Non-Profit Corporation Act. Ownership within a Community Association falls under one of the three (3) types of property ownership:

> **Homeowners Associations** - subdivisions of single-family attached or detached homes.
> **Condominiums** – a form of property ownership, not an architectural style, and is defined as portions of real estate designed for separate ownership and the remainder owned in-common by all owners.
> **Cooperatives** – the members purchase shares of stock in a corporation which owns all property. Stock ownership entitles members to lease a unit.

Understand the Governing Documents and know the laws that govern your property! (CC&R's Covenants, Conditions and Restrictions)

Federal Laws – All corporations have to abide by IRS Federal Tax Laws and Federal Business Laws. It depends on the Associations incorporation documents and the type of property when determining which state laws your association will be required to follow.

A **not-for-profit** may have members who do benefit from the organization's income. A social or recreation club - a not-for-profit - must meet 501(c)(7) requirements; which state that it must be organized for pleasure, recreation and other similar non-profitable purposes.

A member of a **nonprofit** could be an employee or volunteer, neither of whom benefits from the organization's income. Employees of a nonprofit earn salaries that do not depend on the organization's fund raising efforts. Volunteers, by definition, do not benefit from the organization's income. A public charity - a nonprofit - must meet 501(c)(3) requirements; which state that it must be organized and operated exclusively for one of several purposes, including religious, charitable and educational purposes.

State Laws - In South Carolina are...

Non-Profit Corporation Act that governs Non Profit and Not-for-Profit Corporations
Horizontal Property Regime Act that governs Condominium HOA's
The South Carolina Vacation Rental Act that governs Residential Vacation Rentals
(Since many homeowners in Myrtle Beach may rent their home/condo out to vacationers the SC Vacation Rental Act "excludes" lodging provided by hotels, motels, tourist campgrounds, and condominiums with multiple owners who do ANY of the following– rent units on a daily basis or longer; residential rental property on a weekly or monthly basis; timeshares; provide a front desk or office for customer service; OR provide housekeeping services at no additional charge).

The CCR's

Master Deed (Covenants) – The document explaining the creation of the association. It explains the % of common elements to each unit and includes the By Laws.

By Laws (Conditions) – Explains the duties, responsibilities and operation of the association.

Rules and Regulations (Restrictions) – Carry out the duties and responsibilities listed in the By Laws.

Roberts Rules of Order – Rules on how to gather and assemble in meetings. Many Associations adopt these rules and if so will be stated in the By-Laws.

Laws tell you what you have to do, But now you have to plan and follow them!

Lesson 5: BUSINESS 101: Planning
The Operation Plan & Project Management

Understand that the BOARD must PLAN and DEVELOP the Practices, Processes and Procedures for the HOA

Today's buyers are savvy and smart investors. They will avoid buying into Homeowners Associations where common areas are not presentable and community budgets show cost overruns and special assessments for unplanned repairs. Therefore, it is to the HOA's benefit and that of all its homeowners to maintain the property and to establish a budget to allow for a reserve for unplanned repairs. Planning is vital to the success of the HOA and the Board needs to fully understand OPERATION **PLANNING and Project Management**. **Operation Planning is** the process of setting goals and objectives and determining what should be done to accomplish them. The objectives for the board will be a list of the specific results that the board wishes to achieve. When the board does <u>not</u> have a PLAN they will begin to see problems manifest.

The OPERATION PLAN is a working document.
It will assist the Board by...
1. **Mapping out tasks in order of importance**
2. **Allowing for time to explore options**
3. **Permitting the Board to make the best decision for the association**

Easy to design...
The plan can be an Excel Spreadsheet, Word Document or simply a written notebook --- <u>anything is better than NOTHING!</u> It should be revisited regularly (at least quarterly and when new board members are elected) to make sure it is continually updated and objectives has remain the same.

It is vital that the Association or Community has a complete **OPERATION PLAN** in place to avoid problems. Below are the benefits of an Operation plan and the different types of plans the board will need to develop.

Benefits of a Plan:
1. **Direction and focus**
2. **Enables you to be aware of the advantages of an organized plan and it will assist the HOA Board in…**
   a. Prioritizing – Most important (hierarchy of objective)
   b. Identifying problems and opportunities
   c. Learning to accept change and be able to implement an alternative
   d. Better time management

Types of Plans:
1. **Short-range:** Covers one year or less <Intermediate 1-2 years?>.
2. **Long-range:** Covers three or more years.
3. **Strategic:** Comprehensive and detailed; utilized for long term goals and also identifies financial resources in detail. (see 4 through 7)

(The following plans #4 through #7 are performed to assist in completing PLAN #3)

4. **Operational:** What needs to be done in specific areas to obtain the objective of the strategic plan? Leads into plans for each area.
5. **Budget:** Plan to allocate funds needed for each specific project or event. Equipment, hiring employees, hiring outside consultants, also future resources for long term goals (strategic plan).
6. **Procedural:** Guidelines and rules dealing with specific situations. A "policy handbook" or SOP (standard operating procedures) is the outcome of this plan.
7. **Project Schedule:** Define the task, start date, completion date and the timetable to perform specific activities, such as, project specifications, bid announcement, and special assessments.

As the plans develop the board will be in various stages of planning from certainty (alternatives are known), risk (information is not complete or known) and uncertainty (information is poor and alternatives are hard to analyze as outcome).

Now that you understand Operation Planning, let's define **PROJECT MANAGEMENT**.
Project management is the application of knowledge, skills and techniques to execute projects effectively and efficiently. The project results should coincide with the HOA's goals.

Projects are:
1. A temporary group of activities designed to produce a unique product, service or result.
2. Considered temporary activities for it has a defined beginning and end in time, and therefore defined scope and resources.
3. Unique in that it is not a routine operation but a specific set of operations designed to accomplish a singular goal.
4. Planned team efforts that can include many members, board members with the experience to provide input into the project, consultants, onsite personnel or outside contractors.
5. Expertly managed to deliver the on-time, on-budget results, learning and integration that organizations need.

*When the Board **DOESN'T** have plans this happens…*
- **The Board member is assigned multiple duties and responsibilities**
- **The Board jumps from one issue/project to another without considering the long term effect**
- **The Board is in reactive mode instead of proactive mode**

*When the BOARD **DOES** have plans they can expect…*
- **to become a team and be able to reach it goals more quickly**
- **to become focused and know exactly what needs done, WHEN & WHY and COSTS**
- **to be better able to forecast community needs**
- **to communicate more effectively and informatively**

How well is your HOA board doing with Planning, Decision Making, Controlling the Results and Preparing for Daily Projects and Capital Projects?

The honest answer to that question will mostly likely be either not too well, if you are on a board that plans, or we don't have plans. Most boards don't plan and instead take a "JIT" approach to handling board business and projects. JIT –Just in Time –means the board is handling business and projects as an issue arises with no plan in place. If this is your board you need to change the boards "paradigm" and way of thinking. It is vital to the success of your board and community that the development of an Operation plan and Project plans are designed and implemented. Below are the steps necessary for Operation Planning and Project Management; making decisions and controlling the outcomes. Good luck and have fun learning by applying the following steps!

Planning is a 5 Step Process

1. Define the HOA Board's objectives
    a. Results
    b. Where you want to go
    c. What do you want to do
    d. Set benchmarks – timeline (Benchmarking: External comparisons to evaluate current and future performance and actions)
2. Determine where the board is with objectives
    a. Evaluate current results
    b. Identify strengths and weaknesses
3. Determine future conditions
    a. Anticipate future events (Forecasting: Models used to predict future)
    b. For each event identify what will happen and what will help or hinder the plan
4. Analyze alternatives (Back-up plan)
    a. List alternatives
    b. Evaluate each alternative
    c. Choose the one that will best meet your objective(s)
    d. Write step-by-step action plan
5. Implement the plan and evaluate
   Participative Planning-Ask for help from members who will be involved
    a. Put your plan into action
    b. Encourage and note feedback
    c. Evaluate results
    d. Make changes as necessary

Contingency Planning-Identify alternative course of action to take when circumstances change the outcome.

Decision Making is a 5 Step Process

1. Identify that a problem exists; define the problem
    a. Look beyond symptoms; get to the root – the cause!
    b. Be detailed in explaining and defining the problem, so alternatives can be identified
2. Identify solutions and course of action
    a. Collect information and analyze
    b. List alternatives and the course of action
    c. List pros and cons of each alternative/action
    d. Identify any costs associated with the alternative/action
    e. Analyze the benefits of each alternative/action
    f. Analyze time needed to implement

3. Choose the alternative/course of action
    a. Select best alternative
    b. Inform your organization as to why this is needed and that you need their involvement
    c. Be prepared for resistance to change
4. Implement the alternative/course of action
5. Evaluate results
    a. Encourage feedback throughout the organization
    b. Listen and react
    c. Alter plan where necessary and be willing to disregard and start over <most of the time need only to review step-by-step process to catch error>

Know the Decision Makers within the Community ---are they...

Analytic – use systems to evaluate & narrow alternatives. Use methods, step-by-step procedures, rely on graphs, models & mathematical relationships.

OR

Heuristic – use aids of some guidelines. They are experience based (past experience or experience of others) and use when timely information is difficult to acquire.

Both types of Decision Makers deal with the Decision Support System (DSS) which has 3 phases of problem solving and help in each.

1. **Intelligence Phase** – aware problem exists, searches external & internal environments that call for action.
2. **Design Phase** – analyzes alternative solutions & generates alternatives.
3. **Choice Phase** – chooses a solution to solve problem.

Controlling (Results & Outcomes) is a 4 Step Process

1. **Establish Objective and Standards**
   Output Standard: Measures in terms of quantity, quality, cost or time
   Input Standard: Measures work efforts that go into a performance task

2. **Measuring Performance**
    a. Must be accurate
    b. Must be consistent

3. Comparing Results with Objective and Standards
(This comparison will determine if a corrective action is needed)

Desired Performance - Actual Performance = Need for Action

Historical Comparison: Uses past performances
Relative Comparison: Uses performance of other persons work units of organizations
Engineering Comparison: Use set standards such as through methods of the time and motion studies

4. Taking Corrective Action

This allows for *Management by Exception*, which is the practice of giving priority attention to situations that show the greatest need for action.

- An ineffective board member/manager makes a decision and takes action, and then forgets about it and moves onto something else
- An effective board member/manager makes sure everything is working and their control is:
    1. Strategic and result oriented – support the Strategic Plan
    2. Understandable-terms are easy to understand
    3. Encourages self-control-allows for good communication
    4. Timely and exception oriented-quick and addresses performance gaps and what is needed
    5. Positive-emphasizes change and contributions
    6. Fair and Objective – impartial, accurate and uses performance enhancement
    7. Flexible – leaves room for modification

Now that the board has an effective Operation plan in place, and fully understands Project Management when addressing the daily problems that arise within the community, it is time to concentrate on long term goals. The future capital needs of the property. These needs are identified in a study of the property and although called by many names, Reserve Study, Life Cycle Study and/or Feasibility Study, it is vital to the board to get the study done. Most importantly, the board needs to adhere to the recommendations that the consultant/engineer identified in the study.

Reserve Study, Life Cycle Study, and Feasibility Study (called many things)

- The study will look at future capital needs of the property. Example: new roof, new windows, new security or fire alarm system, etc.
- Typically done by a third party company. This company will list in priority the deficiencies, the projected time line and estimated replacement costs. The cost of the study can run from $500 to $5000 or more depending on the community size and need.
- The study helps the HOA Board plan and budget for capital budgets.

Question: Is your HOA Board wondering if they should reduce or stop funding reserves To ease the burden on their Homeowners?

Answer: NO! Better yet, can you? What do your governing documents say about your reserve funds?

FEASIBILITY STUDY –Feasibility study should be performed to determine both a need for the Improvement and is it Practical. It is never an easy task and should include:
1. TECHNICAL FEASIBILITY – find out whether the current technical resources can be updated or added to before introducing a new system.
2. ECONOMICAL FEASIBILITY – consider the board's time and that of the entire community. Also look at the cost of doing a full systems study (which includes time of employees you will be working with and the cost of those business employees' time) the estimated cost of hardware and the estimated cost of software and possible software development, external specialist = calculate if within budget.
3. OPERATIONAL FEASIBILITY – dependent on the human resources available for the project. It involves projecting whether the change will operate once it is implemented.

FIVE CRITERIA FOR PROJECT SELECTION:
1. Backing from homeowners - nothing can be accomplished without the endorsement of the people who eventually will approve and follow the suggestions.
2. Timing – the board must decide if the budget/community/board is presently capable of making a time commitment to correct the problem.
3. Improvement – solving the problem should either put the community on target – or move them ahead of the board's goals and objectives.
4. Practical – solving the problem.
5. Select the best solution – look at all alternatives and stand by the board's selection.

FUNDING THE CAPITAL PROJECT:
When funding the capital project the HOA Board usually looks at either (1) funding by drawing on reserves (2) funding by borrowing from the bank or (3) funding by doing a special assessment. **BUT…lets shift your paradigm**

WHAT ABOUT
Having the Contractor fund a %
OR
GETTING GOVERNMENT GRANTS

GRANTS awarded to HOA's in Washington:

- $16,347 to the Maple Ridge Homeowners Association to erect a new playground structure in their common area.
- $10,000 for the Brookfield Homeowners Association for the planting of trees and the installation of an irrigation system at the three islands leading to the neighborhood.
- Shamrock Heights HOA was given $6,029 to install an entry sign at the main entrance to their neighborhood.
- LaCrosse Homeowners Association will receive $5,789 to erect a neighborhood kiosk in their common area and to add signs and landscaping to entrances.
- Monterey Terrace Neighborhood Association will get $4,321 to landscape the steep slopes at the entrance to their neighborhood as a way to combat erosion.

Look at yourself as an officer in a business. The 3P's!

Practices will develop into Processes

Processes will develop into Procedures/Policies

**Procedures/Policies will develop into
*Rules & Regulations!***

Lesson 6: The Association's 3P's: Practices –

The performance of the day-to-day functions!

Certain business practices in the HOA should be performed, such as:

1. **Use HOA Letterhead:** Managers using HOA letterhead instead of management company letterhead for the HOA correspondence will avoid confusion as to who the true party in authority is. For example, in a contract dispute, the contractor should be clear that the contract is with the HOA and not with the managing company.

2. **Board Signs Contracts:** Managers should have the board sign all contracts. That way, the board is always aware of the contracts and the manager is not subject to questioning whether there was authority to enter into the contract.

3. **Bank Accounts:** No rules exist on the exact number of bank accounts the HOA needs. Some are required, such as normal operating bank account, the reserve account and the trust account if deposits or rents are being collected. One recommendation is to limit the signatory on bank accounts and a good practice is not more than two signatures of board members and the Association Manager if one exists. Sometimes the signatory requirement is dictated by the bank which may require three (3) or four (4) signatures.

    Some suggestions:
    A. Open a bank account when a Special Assessment is required.
    B. Investment accounts may be smart if the reserve balance is extremely large. Some HOA's open up CD's or invest with brokers.

4. **Owners Aging In-Place:** As the population within the community ages the Association will most likely face new challenges. Aging in place affects all aspects of the community; social, operational and in governing. The practice of "Aging In-place" is becoming more and more common. Furthermore, the rights and privacy of your elderly owners need to be considered. Especially when they begin suffering from dementia, physical incapacitation or inadequate support and the Association has to preserve the rights of those owners' neighbors.

    The Association may see:
    A. Issues that relate to an owner needing more handicapped accommodations.
    B. Board governance issue that needs to address a board member with early-stage dementia or Alzheimer's.
    C. Increased complaints of wandering, declining hygiene, etc.
    D. Need for additional services, such as assistance with moving out, getting mail, etc.

    Some suggestions:
    - Add Aging Population sections, policies and procedures into your governing documents. Name the responsible person or team that will make the decision when a

homeowner can no longer care for them self. This will be necessary when the family does not or the homeowner has no family.
- Develop a "Care for your Neighbor" Committee
- Make sure you have family contact information and document all notifications to the family.

Statistics from the white paper "Aging in Place" August 2013 by Dr. James Johnson, Jr. and Dr. Allan Parnell
- 23.9% of the population in SC are over 65
- 30% of an increase in the senior population from 2010 to 2012
- 40% of that increase was seen in Horry County

5. **Risk Management/Outsource Security Guards:** Boards and Businesses are getting wise to the fact that Security Services are becoming too costly and liability is one of the most important issues to examine. Therefore, outsourcing is the way to go.

Here are five good reasons why:
- Lowers your overall cost and liability. Health and liability insurance is very costly for Security Personnel.
- Human Resource Administration reduced: the hiring, scheduling, and the management of the daily operation of the Security division are very stressful.
- Expertise: Security firm's staff is highly trained, qualified and has the certification requirements to perform the duties.
- Flexibility: Security guard companies have the ability to provide coverage for shift call-offs or emergency situations.
- Impartiality: Outsourcing Security reduces the accusations of bias and/or favoritism within the community.

6. **If Possible, Create a Wellness/Fitness Initiative**: Many HOA's have exercise facilities, pools, saunas and/or steam rooms and do not offer a health fitness or wellness program. Some offer no fitness assistance or guidance, while others have a DIY management program "Doing it yourself" and others outsource for assistance. Outsourcing is expensive; however, it spreads out the risk and costs can be either direct or indirect. Many HOA's charge a small fee to their homeowners to offset costs. You would be surprised how

many owners sign up for water aerobics classes, exercise coaching and experienced direction to deal with health issues.

7. **Have Adequate Staffing**: Remember to treat your HOA as a business. Confirm that the Management Company is adequately staffed to service your community. This is usually done by reviewing sound formulas and benchmarks available in the field of Facility Management and staffing. One benchmark was the International Facility Management Association (IFMA) 2005 survey of over 650 Operations and Maintenance organizations. This survey resulted in benchmarks that were tabulated in IFMA's Operations and Maintenance Benchmarks Research Report #26. The outcome is included below. The report lists overall maintenance staffing levels based on facility size and a staffing ratio of one maintenance FTE per 47,000 rentable Square feet.

Overall Maintenance Staffing

Facility Size (RSF)	N	Total Maintenance Staff
Less than 50,000	44	3.00
50,000 to 100,000	97	5.08
100,001 to 250,000	143	7.53
250,001 to 500,000	124	9.00
500,001 to 750,000	51	11.50
750,001 to 1,000,000	39	25.50
1,000,001 to 1,500,000	31	34.74
1,500,001 to 2,000,000	11	38.23
2,000,001 to 3,000,000	8	51.50
More than 3,000,000	19	155.00

Staffing ratio – 1 Maintenance FTE per 47,000 RSF
N = Number of facilities in that RSF that supplied input into the survey
Source: IFMA's Operations and Maintenance Benchmarks Research Report #26

Lesson 7: The Association's 3P's: Processes –

Methods on how Business should be conducted!
Certain processes need to be conducted in certain ways and methods, such as:

1. **Develop a Process for Emails:** An email <u>is not</u> considered Intellectual Property unless the email **includes an original derivative work by the author** of the email. Laws exist that permit the receiver of an email to share the email without the permission of the owner/sender, such as**:** Copyright law, **which states that if the email is NOT an original derivative work and the** Fair Use Exception applies, **which is an email that contains information that can inform or educate, or be used as research the email is not Intellectual Property and can be shared.**
   Copyright protection is for original derivative works.
   http://copyright.gov/title17/92chap1.pdf
   Fair USE exception http://www.ehow.com/list_6834928_email-copyright-laws.html

   Subject Matter and Scope of Copyright -§101 Copyright Law of the United States
   (3) A work is "created" when it is fixed in a copy or phonograph record for the first time; where a work is prepared over a period of time, the portion of it that has been fixed at any particular time constitutes the work as of that time, and where the work has been prepared in different versions, each version constitutes a separate work. A "derivative work" is a work based upon one or more preexisting works, such as a translation, musical arrangement, dramatization, fictionalization, motion picture version, sound recording, art reproduction, abridgment, condensation, or any other form in which a work may be recast, transformed, or adapted. A work consisting of editorial revisions, annotations, elaborations, or other modifications, which, as a whole, represent an original work of authorship.
   http://www.copyright.gov/fls/fl102.html

2. **Create a Professional Board Meeting Agenda:** Spend time on the Agenda. This is a common mistake that many boards make when preparing for meetings.
   A properly created agenda should have a VISION that has the following uses:
   - A. Energizes the meeting
   - B. Provides direction
   - C. Provides a purpose
   - D. Manages the meeting

     Responsibilities of the President of the Board of Directors:
     - Creates the Agenda.
     - Solicits issues and ideas from other board officers and committee chairs.
     - Compile the Agenda based on the input that was shared.
     - Topics placed on the Agenda should be well researched.
     - Assure that all supporting data is ready to be copied and/or distributed. Make sure the handouts have no spelling errors and are correct before copying.
     - Agenda should be manageable and obtainable.

Pointers:
- Consider developing a "Consent Agenda" this is an Agenda that allows for items to be voted on as a whole. Example: management issues/approvals, authorizing banking transfers, minor procedural changes, etc. Any item not requiring explanation or board discussions. There will be one motion to approve the "Consent Agenda" but it will take only one vote from any one board member to remove any item from the consent agenda before the vote to have it moved to the regular Agenda. If using "Consent Agenda" you will have one Agenda to distribute but have them separated on the handout.
- Make sure you have times allotted to items for discussion. The time limit can be stretched, but only if the entire group agrees.
- Urgent issues are always first.
- If an Agenda item requires action or motion –allow sufficient time for discussion. Make sure the time allotted includes the time for clarification and any opposing points of view.
- If an item needs energy or fresh ideas put it near the beginning of the Agenda.
- When a controversial issue is up for discussion "sandwich" it in between less controversial topics.
- Don't dwell long on trivial items –place a time to discuss and hold to it.
- Minimize oral reports of old business by requiring a written report.
- Focus on the future
- List the name of the responsible person introducing the issue on the Agenda.
- Try and end the meeting with a unifying issue.

3. **Conduct Effective Board Meetings: USE** Robert's Rules of Order. Most HOA's have them included in their By-Laws and when they do –follow them!

Meeting Guidelines
- Obtain the floor (the right to speak) by being the first to stand when the person speaking has finished; state Mr. /Madam Chairman. Raising your hand means nothing, and standing while another has the floor is out of order! Must be recognized by the Chair before speaking!
- Debate cannot begin until the Chair has stated the motion or resolution and asked "are you ready for the question?" If no one rises, the chair calls for the vote!
- Before the motion is stated by the Chair (the question) members may suggest modification of the motion; the mover can modify as he pleases, or even withdraw the motion without consent of the seconder; if mover modifies, the seconder can withdraw the second.
- The "immediately pending question" is the last question stated by the Chair! Motion/Resolution - Amendment - Motion to Postpone
- The member moving the "immediately pending question" is entitled to preference to the floor!
- No member can speak twice to the same issue until everyone else wishing to speak has spoken to it once!
- All remarks must be directed to the Chair. Remarks must be courteous in language and deportment - avoid all personalities, never allude to others by name or to motives!

- The agenda and all committee reports are merely recommendations! When presented to the assembly and the question is stated, debate begins and changes occur!

The Rules
- **Point of Privilege:** Pertains to noise, personal comfort, etc. - may interrupt only if necessary!
- **Parliamentary Inquiry:** Inquire as to the correct motion - to accomplish a desired result, or raise a point of order.
- **Point of Information:** Generally applies to information desired from the speaker: "I should like to ask the (speaker) a question."
- **Orders of the Day** (Agenda): A call to adhere to the agenda (a deviation from the agenda requires Suspending the Rules).
- **Point of Order:** Infraction of the rules, or improper decorum in speaking. Must be raised immediately after the error is made.
- **Main Motion:** Brings new business (the next item on the agenda) before the assembly
- **Divide the Question:** Divides a motion into two or more separate motions (must be able to stand on their own).
- **Consider by Paragraph:** Adoption of paper is held until all paragraphs are debated and amended and entire paper is satisfactory: After all paragraphs are considered the entire paper is then open to amendment, and paragraphs may be further amended. Any Preamble cannot be considered until debate on the body of the paper has ceased.
- **Amend:** Inserting or striking out words or paragraphs, or substituting whole paragraphs or resolutions.
- **Withdraw/Modify Motion:** Applies only after question is stated; mover can accept an amendment without obtaining the floor.
- **Commit /Refer/Recommit to Committee:** State the committee to receive the question or resolution; if no committee exists, include size of committee desired and method of selecting the members (election or appointment).
- **Extend Debate:** Applies only to the immediately pending question; extends until a certain time or for a certain period of time.
- **Limit Debate:** Closing debate at a certain time or limiting to a certain period of time.
- **Postpone to a Certain Time:** State the time the motion or agenda item will be resumed.
- **Object to Consideration:** Objection must be stated before discussion or another motion is stated.
- **Lay on the Table:** Temporarily suspends further consideration/action on pending question; may be made after motion to close debate has carried or is pending.
- **Take from the Table:** Resumes consideration of item previously "laid on the table" - state the motion to take from the table.
- **Reconsider:** Can be made only by one on the prevailing side who has changed position or view.
- **Postpone Indefinitely:** Kills the question/resolution for this session. Exception the motion to reconsider can be made this session.
- **Previous Question:** Closes debate if successful - may be moved to **"Close Debate"** if preferred.

- **Informal Consideration:** Move that the assembly go into **"Committee of the Whole"** - informal debate as if in committee; this committee may limit number or length of speeches or close debate by other means by a 2/3 vote. All votes, however, are formal.
- **Appeal Decision of the Chair:** Appeal for the assembly to decide - must be made before other business is resumed; NOT debatable if relates to decorum, violation of rules or order of business.
- **Suspend the Rules:** Allows a violation of the assembly's own rules (except Constitution); the object of the suspension must be specified.

© 1997 Beverly Kennedy

"I move that we debate whether to vote to decide whether to discuss bringing this meeting to an end."

4. **Recording the Meeting Minutes:** Remember meeting minutes are written records of the actions taken at a meeting NOT what was SAID. In other words minutes are not written narratives of every comment made at a meeting.

Pointers:
- Design a form (template) to use when taking the minutes. This template should follow the outline of the agenda and include the sections listed below. Even when a recording device is used it is a good idea to take long hand, written minutes as a backup. If a meeting is canceled for any reason complete the form, note why it was canceled and put it into the Minute Book of Records. (This way it confirms that meeting minutes are not missing)
- Minutes act as the legal record of what was decided, voted on and the business conducted at a meeting.

- Minutes become official when they are approved at the next meeting, signed by the Secretary and placed in the Minute Book of Records. The official copy should have the copies of the original reports attached. (Reports from Committees, Officers, Written Motions, and Policies approved, etc.) When copies of the minutes are distributed at the meetings the copies of the reports are not included, but are referenced and instructions on how to obtain copies should be noted.
- If the Agenda is well written and followed the composing of the minutes should be a quick and efficient mission.

Roberts's Rules Recommend the Following Sections be INCLUDED:
- Name of the Organization
- Type of Meeting (Regular/Special)
- Date, Time and Place
- Name of Presiding Officer (Usually the President of the BOD)
- Name of the Recorder of the Minutes
- Board Members Present
- Board Members Absent
- Establishment of a Quorum
- Record of Actions: Who made a motion and if the motion passed or failed
- Record Board Members Name of any Dissenting or Abstained Votes
- Reports: Name of reporting member and type of report.

Robert's Rules Recommend the Following be EXCLUDED:
- Opinions, Interpretations, Judgmental Comments, or Detailed Discussions
- Motions that are withdrawn
- No need to list who seconded a motion
- Transcripts of the meeting

5. Follow ADA Standards for Accessible Parking Spaces:
Review the Illustrations and Guidance documents on the following websites.
U.S. Access Board Parking Technical Bulletin http://www.access-board.gov/adaag/about/bulletins/parking.htm
U.S. Department of Justice - ADA Business Brief - Re-striping Parking Lots
http://www.ada.gov/restribr.htm

Accessible parking space must:
1. Allow for at least 96 inches (8 feet) wide and shall have an adjacent access aisle.
2. Have an access aisle adjacent to all Van-accessible parking spaces that measure 96-inches (8 feet) wide, and a 60-inch (5 feet) wide access aisle adjacent to the parking space for standard accessible parking spaces.
3. Permit the accessible path of travel from the parking space to the building start from the access aisle.
4. Access aisles are to be kept clear of all obstructions at all times.
5. Have the Accessible parking space be designated by a sign per **NH RSA 265: 73-a**.

Codes require that the sign display of the Universal Symbol of Accessibility and be mounted on a post or on a building wall so that the bottom of the sign is at least 60 inches above the surface of the parking space. Signs are to be located at the head of each accessible parking space. *Please do not use signs that have text with any form of The word "handicapped."*

6. Have the Access aisles marked with diagonal stripes, preferably yellow, and are to be part of the accessible route to the building. If possible, a "NO PARKING" sign should be installed.

Technical Requirements are:
1. Refer to IBC 2006 Section 1106, ANSI A117.1 Sections 502 And 503, and the ADA Standards for Accessible Design, Sections 4.1.2 and 4.6.
2. Accessible parking spaces must be located on the shortest accessible route of travel from the parking to an accessible building entrance. In parking facilities that do not serve a particular building, accessible parking spaces must be located on the shortest route to an accessible pedestrian entrance to the parking facility. Where buildings have multiple accessible entrances with adjacent parking, accessible parking spaces shall be dispersed and located near the accessible entrances. This usually means that the minimum number of accessible parking spaces must be exceeded in order to provide equal access to multiple entrances.
3. The amount of accessible parking spaces that must be provided is based on the total number of spaces in each parking lot, *see table below*. At least one parking space must be van-accessible and for every 6 (six) accessible parking spaces, there must be one van-accessible space.

Total Parking Spaces Provided	Required Minimum Number of Accessible Spaces
1 to 25	1
26 to 50	2
51 to 75	3
76 to 100	4
101 to 150	5
151 to 200	6
201 to 300	7
301 to 400	8
401 to 500	9
501 to 1,000	2% of Total
More than 1,000	20 +1 for each 100 over 1,000

Lesson 8: The Association's 3P's: Procedures/Policies – Step by Step Lessons on how the HOA will operate! Creating policies will develop into written rules we call the *Rules & Regulations*!

Remember the HOA is a BUSINESS! Therefore, like any business the HOA will follow the operation plan and practices in place and begin writing policies.

Writing policies will ensure that the HOA will:

1. Be in Compliance with Federal, State, Local and Corporate laws
2. Operate based on the HOA's Goals and Objectives (the plan)
3. Manage Risks
4. Experience Continual Improvement (increase value)

No true format exist for writing policies and many examples can be found on the internet. The Board should include the sections listed below and use any format: as long as it is done, any policy manual is better than none! Although the policy manual has many names, Standard Operating Procedures (SOP), Procedural Manual or Policy Manual they all do the same thing. Record the step-by-step process of performing a function within the community. After writing the policy the Board of Directors of the HOA will pass a motion at the board meeting to approve the POLICY ---once accepted it then becomes an **APROVED POLICY.** It too should be revisited regularly (at least quarterly and when new board members are elected) to make sure it is continually updated and that the policy and practice has remained the same.

Sections of the Policy Format:

Introduction – explanation of who, what and why the policy is being designed.

Responsibility – instructions on who will be responsible for implementing this policy.

Policy - step-by-step explanation and instructions of the procedures required in order to perform the function and/or task.

An Example of a Policy:

| Example of Committee Policy |

Creation of Committee's
(In accordance with Robert's Rules of Order: Article IX; Sections 49-57)

INTRODUCTION
In the HOA environment committees are formed to help assist the Board of Directors in the decision making process and are considered a "working committee", which means they do not assist in confidential or employment matters. The reason for this is that the officers on the Board of Directors are the only members that were elected and have a fiduciary and confidential commitment to the community. The committees should not be assisting with the duties of the officers on the board for they are to have the ability to perform the duties they were elected to perform. Therefore, committees to discuss contracts, bids, budgets, meetings, minutes or employee relations, etc. are confidential and matters discussed among board members.

Here at the resort these "volunteer investigation" committees will be organized to provide support to various operational areas within the _____. Each committee should consist of no more than 5 members, and be a representation of all homeowners of the _____.

RESPONSIBILITY
The committee will be chaired by the Board of Directors who volunteered to oversee that area of operation. The committee will be charged to investigate and discuss various issues and topics within their area to assist in the decision making process. The committees will come to a consensus on the change and/or purchase and the findings will be presented by the chair (the board member) at the next working meeting of the Board of Directors. This process will assist the board in making an intelligent and well informed decision on the topic at hand.

POLICY

COMMITTEE VOLUNTEERS
Committee volunteers will be solicited by sending out an email notice to all _____ homeowners explaining the creation of committees and asking them to volunteer. This will provide all members of the association a fair opportunity to get involved and present a creation of a committee with broad representation and various agendas. The first five emails received for each committee area will create the committee and those individuals will be notified of their appointment by email. The time and date the email is received will act as the official submittal date of receipt. In the event one area receives more than 5 volunteers the homeowner will be asked to join another area that may be lacking, and/or more than 5 committee members may be approved by the President of the Board of Directors. One board member should be appointed as the contact person and receive the email responses. The contact person is usually the Secretary of the Board since he or she is the keeper of the records.

TYPE AND TERM
Standing Committee for a term of One Year
Meetings held via telephone once per month the day and time will be determined at the committee's first meeting.

COMMITTEE MEMBER RULES AND GUIDELINES
In order for the committee to operate efficiently and effectively guidelines and rules must be followed by each member sitting on the committee.

They are as follows:
1. Each Committee member is a volunteer and no compensation or reimbursement for time will be paid.
2. The Committee member should attend via telephone as many monthly meetings as possible. Your contribution and input is necessary to have an effective committee.
3. Meeting Agenda will be distributed by the Chair at least 3 days before a meeting and you should review it to prepare for a constructive committee meeting.
4. Meeting will be chaired by the board member who oversees the area and if he or she cannot hold the meeting than another committee member will be assigned to chair the meeting.
5. Some information and data discussed at the meetings is confidential, such as prices and company information. Therefore, information discussed at a meeting should not be shared with other homeowners without the permission of the board member/chair.

VARIOUS COMMITTEES

BUILDING COMMITTEE: Review which XYZ areas need to be repaired/replaced: review Roofing Contract for changes and make recommendations to the board; review the Building maintenance Contract (if separate) for changes and make recommendations to the board, assist in preparing request for price quotes from roofing/building maintenance contractors when needed, assist in making recommendations to the board on the yearly HOA budget, work with the maintenance contractor in the repair or replacement of the fences.

LANDSCAPE COMMITTEE: Review the trees/bushes etc. on the common area of the _____, and assist in making Improvements. Maintain the signs and work with the social/beautification committee on maintaining the flower gardens. Review the landscape contract, make recommendations for needed changes and assist in preparing the yearly request for price quote for potential contractors. Review the snow removal contract, make recommendations for needed changes and assist in preparing the yearly request for price quote for potential contractors.

ELECTIONS/NOMINATING COMMITTEE: Poll homeowners for new board candidates as necessary. Set up and run the election of new board members at one of the board meetings or at another time if necessary. Work with the board on polling homeowners for volunteering to work on all the HOA committees as necessary

SOCIAL/BEAUTIFICATION COMMITTEE: Put together welcome packets for new homeowners. Work with the Property Manager to provide the packets to the new homeowners.

Put together various seasonal activities/events to promote community goodwill. Maintain the flowers at the kiosks, planters at the signs and the flagpole area. Work with the social committee on holiday decorations. Dig up trees and shrubs not wanted by homeowners. Work with the landscape and planning committee to make recommendations for needed funds for the yearly budget.

INSURANCE COMMITTEE: Review the HOA insurance policies and coverage. Research other companies/agents for competitive prices. Make recommendations to the board. Work with the HOA lawyer as necessary to ensure that claims are received/paid in a reasonable time.

One committee that will be organized is the "**Selection/Search Committee**" when it comes time to select a new management company. Below is a lesson that describes the steps that we have found to be successful when selecting a new management company for a community.

Lesson 9: Selecting the Associations Management Company

The Board Becomes the Visionaries

This section will be helpful to those **HOA Board** members already in office. Remember, the HOA is a business and more so now with these tough economic times the **HOA Board** members must act as **"visionaries"** and become the **VICE Squad!**

> **V** for **Value** of Understanding Your Duties and Property Management
> **I** for the **Importance** of an RFP – Request for Proposal
> **C** for knowing the **Contract** Provision Requirements
> **E** for **Evaluating** and Selecting the Management Company

Learn the various levels of fiduciary duties you have and the various "hats" you wear. Understand that the most important "duty and hat" represents the action of selecting the best management company for the Community. Selecting the company that will meet the wants, needs, and budget constraints the association has to work within.

This is all done through careful and detailed analysis, which in the corporate world is referred to as **Strategic Planning**. In the HOA environment it is usually done in a transparent manner by composing a **"Selection/Search Committee"** of representatives from all regimes, when multiple regimes exist, charged with selecting the best management company for the Community. This committee is composed of board members from each regime not homeowners, for confidential and private business practices will be revealed through this bidding process. This committee needs special skills, such as planning and critical thinking.

The Board Members for this Selection/Search Committee should be able to:
1. Master the skill of *critical thinking* in order to make intelligent and informative decisions.
2. Identify all the *key players*.
3. Understand what extent the key players have in present and future development.

These Board Members must have the skill of Critical Thinking:

Critical Thinking is when the board correctly applies the issues for the topic at hand in a logical and relevant manner. It also includes the following elements:
- Precision: analyzing the topic/issue/problem.
- Breadth: addressing the full breadth and understanding.
- Organization: remaining focused on the issue at hand.
- Clarity: addressing the key concepts in a clear and direct delivery.
- Referencing: inform the members of the location of resources by citing sources.

This Selection/Search Committee is <u>charged</u> with the following steps:
1. The Selection Committee is developed with a board member from each regime, when multiple regimes exist.
2. The committee should begin meeting 4 or 5 months before the present contract expires.
3. This committee solicits bids from many companies inviting them to submit a Request for Proposal (RFP). Solicit many bids for on average only 25% of those invited will respond. So it depends on the number of RFP's your board wants to review.
4. Schedule a tour of the community for those companies that are doing the RFP. Each company should have a private tour. Do not schedule one tour.
5. The RFP's will be reviewed and evaluated by the committee and three (3) companies will be selected based on the three highest scores.

<u>**NOW THE COMMITTEE SHARES WITH THEIR ENTIRE BOD's IN THEIR REGIMES**</u>

6. The committee will share the complete RFP's of the three (3) companies the committee selected with the Board of Directors of their regimes to review. Remember the information provided in these RFP's are private and confidential, so remind the BOD that they are for "their eyes only" and not to be shared with homeowners.
7. The three (3) highest companies will be invited to do a presentation to each BOD of the regime boards.
8. Each Board member will be given an evaluation form on the three (3) companies to complete. After tallying these evaluations each BOD (Regime) will have the order of choice for the three (3) companies selected. Most HOA's with multiple regimes bylaws enable them to select a management company of their choice. Therefore, although not managerially the best practice, but a community can have multiple management companies onsite.
9. The Board will begin negotiations with the highest company (#1) on the list, and will take into consideration the HOA's **vision and the ability to accept change.**

"Basically, we're looking for an innovative pastor with a fresh vision who will inspire our church to remain exactly the same."

V for Value
Understanding Your Duties, And Property Management Planning

(Duties explained earlier in-depth)

Duty of Care
Requires you to act in good faith and make informed decisions

Duty of Loyalty
Requires you to put the interest of the association above your personal interest

Duty to Act within Scope of Authority
Requires you to perform duties you're obligated to carry out

Duties on the Board

Understand Property Management: The term Property Management is a branch of the real estate profession that preserves and increases the value of an investment property while generating income for its investor. The properties are rental leases in a commercial development and the manager who is entrusted to manage the owner's funds and interact with the tenants is called the Property Manager. In South Carolina Property Managers are required to be licensed under the Real Estate Commission. In a Residential HOA the managers are called Community Managers and although they are also entrusted to manage the owner's funds, they are presently not required to be licensed in South Carolina. The goal of both managers is to preserve and increase the value of the property. Therefore, no matter the classification and type of property, the Board members need to develop the Operation plan as discussed earlier.

The OPERATION Plan places "the Board" in the driver seat and directs the association on the "Right" road to travel…

However, the "Management Company" needs to be traveling on the "same" road that the Association wants to go down…

Either way, a professional management company should never run the whole show. It should take its direction from the board. Nor would it be fiscally wise to let an outside firm have full control over your finances. In order to make sure "the board" understands what road the Management Company travels on **DO AN RFP**!

I for Information
The RFP – Request for Proposal

The **HOA Board** has to remember that it is running a **BUSINESS** and in order to be successful must understand that it is a **SYSTEM** that has to learn to develop **SYNERGY**.

System – the components that work together for a common goal.

Synergy – when the interaction of a group of individuals combined produce a total effect that is greater than the sum of the individual person.

The association needs to utilize the "**Request for Proposal" (RFP)** as the document or instrument to invite management companies to bid on managing the HOA's property.

The RFP will assist the association in verbalizing:
- The goals and objectives of the HOA
- The culture within the community
- The business system that is in place

The quality of an **RFP** is very important to successful project management and in this case property management because it clearly describes the deliverables that will be required.

The RFP should include the following sections:
Company Description
- Provide a description of the HOA property.
- Provide the HOA's mission and/or vision.
- Describe the HOA's goals and objectives.

Task Description
- Provide a description of the desired outcome and for whom it is intended. (The Board)
- Stipulate any required templates.
- If requiring special credentials or accreditation, indicate that.
- State the tasks using action verbs such as "design," "develop," "meet," "conduct," "test", "revise," "distribute" and "document." Note any prerequisites or dependencies.
- If your company would entertain the idea of alternative solutions, indicate that as well; such as staffing needs or operational techniques.

Submission Procedure Description
- List the time line and format for the response.
- State the evaluation criteria, such as communication style, location, example quality or other critical concerns.
- Indicate the specifics of what should be included in the proposal, such as cost estimate, staff qualifications, contact information for references.
- Include your contact phone number or other experts so the management company can ask relevant questions before submitting a response.
- State the deadline you impose.
- Request a copy of the management contracts standard managing agreement.

Now that the RFP will be <u>assisting</u> "the Board" with knowing which road the "Management Company" Is traveling on…

"The Board" has to make sure it is the "right" road and will be financially beneficial for the HOA.

In order to understand how smooth the road will be and aware of any potential detours or potholes on the road - **<u>REVIEW AN EXAMPLE OF a CONTRACT/AGREEMENT BEFORE SELECTION</u>**. This will not be the contract from the company who submitted the RFP, they are not yet at that stage. This is an example of a contract, so that the Board can develop a list of questions to ASK when interviewing the potential companies that will be presenting. However, in addition to reviewing an example of a contract for this step, the committee should also be discussing the wording in sections of the contract and what sections they want included and excluded.

C for knowing the Contract Provision Requirements

There is no standard HOA management contract! REMEMBER the Contract/Agreement customarily is written by the management company and <u>will be in the interest of the management company.</u> Some provisions are standard –ONE IMPORTANT provision is INDEMNIFICATION! The Board's job is to protect the association; therefore, be careful if the management contract states that the homeowners association indemnifies the manager in all cases (without regard to negligence, gross negligence or wrongful conduct). This kind of clause is not reasonable and the HOA gives up too many rights.

Common Indemnification Provision:

> **<u>INCLUDE:</u>** The HOA usually wants an indemnification clause which states the HOA shall indemnify the manager from any actions **except for negligence. That makes the manager responsible for negligent acts.** The manager usually wants to increase that standard to gross negligence or willful neglect.
>
> **<u>EXCLUDE:</u>** Sometimes the management contract states that management is liable for gross negligence and willful neglect only if a court decides that the manager is guilty of it. So, **the HOA is obligated to provide the manager's defense** until a court determines that the manager is guilty. Since most cases are settled, this clause gives the manager an additional layer of protection.

Other Common Provisions:

Manager Acting as Employer. For ease of administration, the manager may sometimes act as the employer for employees that, in fact, work for the HOA. The following is one of many reasons why it is good to have the employees be directly employed by the management company and not the HOA.
    Liability
    Workers Compensation Insurance

The Management Agreement. This document should clearly explain the full scope and responsibility of the management companies duties. It should explain that the Senior Property Manager and Community Managers, if they exist, work under the supervision and authority of the board of directors, not independently as members sometimes believe. It is good management principals to have one person be the contact person to the Senior Property Manager who has an office onsite. This eliminates the manager being subjected to numerous "bosses" with many objecting. The chain of command is that all staff reports and takes direction from the Senior Property Manager and/or Community Manager. The

Management Agreement should detail that chain of command and any other issues that require special authority from the board.

Management Companies Insurance: The Management Companies Insurance liability limits need to be clearly defined by your insurance broker. Their insurance <u>must list the association as an additional insured</u>.

The following are provisions *you may find* in a comprehensive HOA management contract.

    1. Appointment and Function of Manager
    1.1. Appointment
    1.2. Duties and Services
    1.3. Independent Contractor Status
    2. Employees of Manager
    3. Duties of Manager
    3.1. General Management
    3.1.1. Counseling
    3.1.2. Development of Policy
    3.1.3. Implementation of Policy
    3.1.4. Compliance with Government Order
    3.1.5. Administration of Personnel
    3.1.6. Enforcement
    3.1.7. Administrative Records
    3.1.8. Solicitation of Proposal for Service
    3.1.9. Contracting
    3.1.10. Insurance Placement and Claims
    3.1.11 Attendance at Meetings
    3.1.12. Meeting Administration
    3.1.13. Financial Records
    3.1.14. Bank Accounts
    3.1.15. Investments
    3.1.16. Collections
    3.1.17. Delinquency Enforcement
    3.1.18. Disbursements
    3.1.19. Financial Statements
    3.1.20. Management Report
    3.1.21. Budget Preparation
    3.1.22. Independent Audit
    3.1.23. Tax Filing
    3.1.24. Record Maintenance and Storage
    3.1.25. Inspection
    3.2. **Property Management**
    3.2.1. Supervision
    3.2.2. Preventative Maintenance
    3.2.3. Inspection
    3.2.4. Work Request Administration
    4. Duties of Association

4.1. Provision and Accuracy of Records
4.2. Provision of Funds
4.3. Provision of Plans
4.4. Designation of Association Principal Place of Business
4.5. Designation of Corporate Contact
4.6. Enforcement

5. Compensation
5.1. Base Management Service
5.2. Additional Management Service
5.3. Resale Certificates, Broker and Lender Requests, Transfer Fees
5.4. Administrative Expenses
5.5. Management Services
5.6. Maintenance Services
5.7. Professional Services

6. Term of Agreement and Termination
6.1. Term
6.2. Termination
6.3. Notice
6.4. Termination Procedure
6.4.1. Turn-over of Records
6.4.2. Termination Accounting
6.5. Expenses Incurred After Termination

7. Liability and Indemnification
7.1. Manager's Liability
7.2. Manager's Insurance
7.3. Association's Insurance
7.4. Placement of Association's Insurance
7.5. Indemnification

8. General Provisions
8.1. Conflict of Interest
8.2. Affiliated Interest
8.3. Modification of Agreement
8.4. Use of Counterparts
8.5. Arbitration
8.6. Jurisdiction
8.7. Void or Unenforceable Terms

E for Evaluating
And Selecting the Management Company

EVALUATION OF PROPOSALS
Proposals are usually evaluated on the following criteria:

1. Financial Assistance Proposal
2. Relevant Experience and Work Quality, substantiated by reference checks
3. Qualifications of Firm/Qualifications of Property Team
4. Compliance with Association's Insurance Coverage –Requirements
5. Compliance with Association's Contractual Requirements
6. Sustainable Business Practices.

OTHER EVALUATING CRITERIA
Presentation to the Board

1. Presentable Appearance
2. Communicates Well
3. PowerPoint, Handouts, and/or Brochures are well Designed and Easy to Understand
4. All Questions are Addressed or the Follow-up Process is Explained

Miscellaneous Business Tools

5. Website Easy to Follow
6. Corporate Office Presentable
7. Feedback is Delivered Quickly and Completely

(If a Company takes the time to present well designed marketing material and the website portrays an easy flow and is informative then that company takes pride in their work)

Future Topics

Book TWO discusses 9 Qualities of Leadership for the HOA

Book THREE will cover Pet Policies and the ADA

"Finally, the first approved pet for homeowner associations."

References:

Cameron, Catherine A. Ph.D.: *777 Business Program*: ISBN-13: 978-1619274112. Also *Business + Technology = Success*: eBook www.amazon.com

Christ, Bruce A., Esq: *Is Your Board Carrying Out Its Fiduciary Duty? Know What that Duty Is & What Constitutes a Breach.*

DeBoaest, Richard II. Esq: *Ten Common Misconceptions about Robert's Rule of Order and how they relate to Community Association Meetings.*

Demand Media, Inc. Fair USE exception http://www.ehow.com/list_6834928_email-copyright-laws.html

HOA Leader: *HOA Leadership Roles and Duties.* 26 pages. www.hoaleader.com, *Master Homeowners Associations: Is Your HOA Its Own Master?* June 2009, http://www.hoaleader.com/public/300.cfm

HOA-USA: *Guide to Understanding Homeowners Association. For association boards, residents, and new home buyers.* Info@hoa-usa.com

International Facility Management Association (IFMA): *IFMA's Operations and Maintenance Benchmarks Research Report #26.* www.ifma.org

Kennedy, Beverly (1997) www.robertsrules.org

Kyle, Robert. C., Spodek, Marie S. DREI, Baird, Floyd M. RPA/SMA: *Property Management.* Ninth Edition, Dearborn Publishing: ISBN-13: 978-427747907

Robert's Rules of Order: *PART IV Meetings and Strategies:* Chapter 16 – Meetings.

Ross, Beth: *Fiduciary Duties of HOA Board Members. How to protect yourself and limit your liability when serving on the board of your homeowners' association.*
http://www.nolo.com/legal-encyclopedia/fiduciary-duties-hoa-board-members.html

South Carolina Code of Laws: *South Carolina Horizontal Property Act*
www.scstatehouse.gov/code/t27c031.php

South Carolina Code of Laws: *South Carolina Non Profit Act*
www.scstatehouse.gov/code/t33c031.php

South Carolina –State Ethics Commission: *Statement of Organization User Guide.* 37 pages. Version 1.01.02 in partnership with SC.GOV

U.S. Access Board Parking Technical Bulletin: http://www.access-board.gov/adaag/about/bulletins/parking.htm

U.S. Department of Justice - ADA Business Brief - Re-striping Parking Lots:

> http://www.ada.gov/restribr.htm

United States Copyright Office. http://copyright.gov/title17/92chap1.pdf, **-§101 Copyright Law of the United States** and http://www.copyright.gov/fls/fl102.html

Webster Online Dictionary: www.webster-dictionary.org

Dr. Cameron's Closing Comments:
My full bio can be found on www.cameronseminars.com. I hope you found this information helpful and it guides you onto your road to success. As a special "thank you" please visit my website and select a FREE copy of your choice of either…

7 Cameron Clue's
Learn to Listen to Lead
DISC Factor Analysis

Learn what you need to SUCCEED!
Dr. Cathy Cameron

Cameron Seminars and Consulting, LLC www.cameronseminars.com can bring a seminar to your HOA board or business.

Books can be purchased on the web and they include **Business + Technology = Success** (which can be found on Amazon or purchase the CD on the website) or a hard copy of the book **777 Business Program.** Find additional HOA seminars and books on **www.Amazon.com.**

William D. Cameron, Co-Author:

Bill has over 40 years of industry experience in facility and operations management. He held the position of Vice President of Operations for Point Park University in Pittsburgh, Pennsylvania where he provided leadership and direction to the departmental areas of Planning, Project Management, Physical Plant, Transportation, Event Planning, Mailroom/Receiving and Public Safety with approximately 100 direct or indirect reports. Bill retired in 2013 to his home in Myrtle Beach that he has owned with Cathy since 1995. Bill earned the reputation for achieving extreme productivity in meeting operations and production objectives, demonstrating exceptional skill when working under pressure, taking the initiative in judgment and decision making and ensuring compliance with all safety, quality and industry standards: all while working within the budget. His extensive training in specialized areas and education at the Institute of Real Estate Management (IREM) Certified Property Management Program provided input and direction in various areas of this training manual.

You can purchase William's **poster** found on the back cover.

Thank you to Thomas W. Winslow for his legal review of this work. To Contact him please find him below:

Thomas Winslow
Attorney At Law

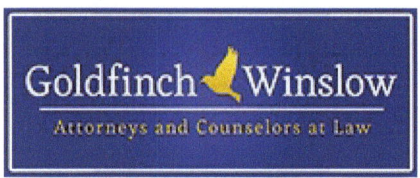

Phone: (843)357-9301
Mobile: (843)655-7333
Fax: (843)357-9303
E-mail: tom@goldfinchwinslow.com
Website: www.goldfinchwinslow.com

www.ingramcontent.com/pod-product-compliance
Lightning Source LLC
Chambersburg PA
CBHW051221220526
45473CB00003B/1120